Easy MAGIC

Jon Day

Illustrated by
Chris Fisher

Contents

All about easy magic	2
Flyaway money	4
Snap!	6
Mint on a string	8
The magic bottle	10
The vanishing key	12
The floating pencil	14
Match me if you can!	16
Reely tricky	18
Magic bangle	20
A knotty problem	22
Finger on the pulse	24

Kingfisher Books

All about easy magic

This book shows you how to do eleven great tricks with everyday objects – matches, bits of string, empty bottles and other things you should be able to find easily at home. On these two pages you can discover some tips and hints to help you become a successful magician.

Practise in front of a mirror to get an audience's eye view.

Hints

1 Make sure you have all the equipment ready and in the right place before you start to do a trick.

2 Resist the temptation to tell your friends how a trick works – even if they are begging you to tell them! Keep them guessing, and that way they will be even more impressed with your skill.

3 Never perform the same trick more than once. That makes it too easy for your friends to work out how it was done.

Safety warning: Be sensible when doing tricks involving matches. Use only spent matches, that have already been burned. Keep all matches and matchboxes away from younger children.

Write yourself a performing script – and learn it by heart. You could record it on tape and listen to it over and over again until you get it right.

The tricks in this book are called 'easy' because they all involve easily found objects, and they are all quite simple to understand. But don't forget that even the simplest trick can astound people if you perform it smoothly and confidently!

Magicians know that there are two things needed to make good magic. The first is **practice.** Work at each trick until you can do it easily and with confidence. That accounts for about ten per cent of a magician's success.

Ninety per cent of a magician's success comes from the way the trick is done – the **presentation.** That means knowing how to act, what to say, and how to persuade people to see only what you want them to see. That's the really tricky bit!

Flyaway money

Things you need

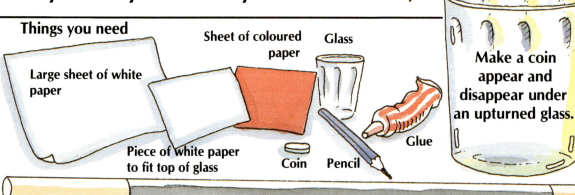

Make a coin appear and disappear under an upturned glass.

Get ready...

Make a paper lid and a cover for the glass.

1 Put the upturned glass on the smaller piece of white paper and draw round the top with a pencil.

2 Cut out the circle and stick it to the top of the glass with glue. Trim it so it fits exactly.

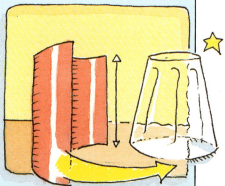

3 Cut a strip of coloured paper the same height as the glass. Bend it round the glass.

4 Stick the edges together to make a cover for the glass. Make sure it slips on and off it easily.

Make sure the cover slips on and off the glass easily.

5 Spread the large white sheet of paper on the table where you are going to perform.

Trick time

1 Put the upturned glass, the coloured paper cover and the coin on the large sheet of white paper.

2 Put the coloured paper cover over the glass.

3 Pick up the cover and the glass together and place them over the coin.

4 Lift off the paper cover – and the coin has vanished!

5 To make the coin reappear, reverse the process. Put the cover over the glass and lift both to one side. There's the coin! Now remove the cover.

Don't let anyone see the paper lid on the glass!

Snap!

Things you need

Handkerchief with a deep hem

2 matchsticks

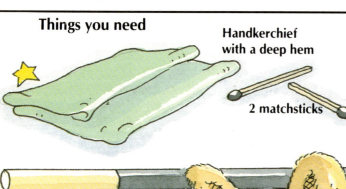

Break a matchstick in two – and then make it whole again.

Get ready . . .

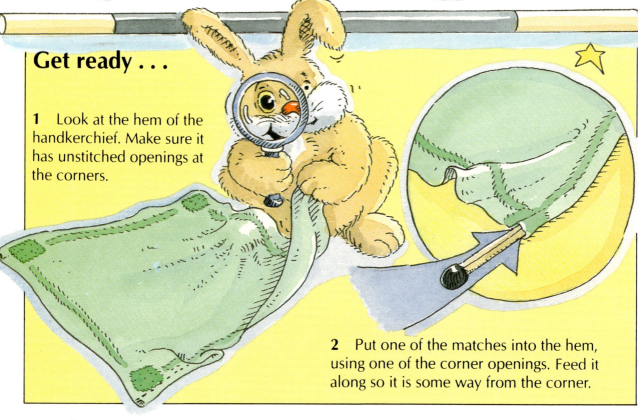

1   Look at the hem of the handkerchief. Make sure it has unstitched openings at the corners.

2   Put one of the matches into the hem, using one of the corner openings. Feed it along so it is some way from the corner.

Trick time

1   Put the handkerchief on the table, making sure the corner containing the match is nearest to you.

2   Put the other match on the centre of the handkerchief.

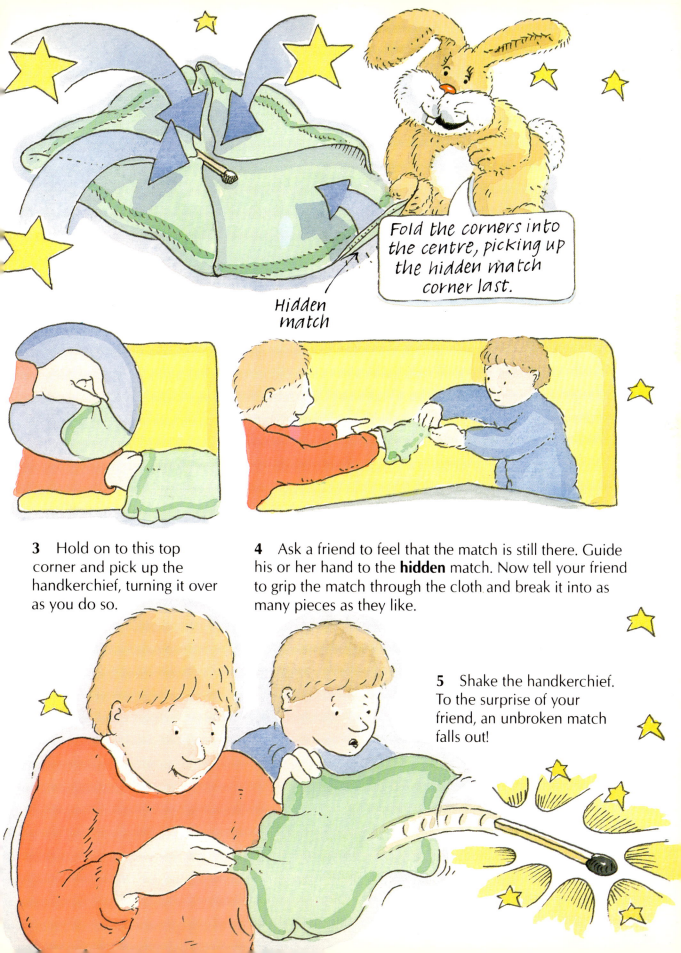

Fold the corners into the centre, picking up the hidden match corner last.

Hidden match

3 Hold on to this top corner and pick up the handkerchief, turning it over as you do so.

4 Ask a friend to feel that the match is still there. Guide his or her hand to the **hidden** match. Now tell your friend to grip the match through the cloth and break it into as many pieces as they like.

5 Shake the handkerchief. To the surprise of your friend, an unbroken match falls out!

Mint on a string

Things you need

Packet of mints

Handkerchief or cloth

Piece of string about 1 metre long

Magically remove a mint from the string it's threaded on!

Get ready...

First make a special trick mint.

If the join shows, rub a little icing sugar into it!

1 Snap a mint in half, making sure you get a nice clean break.

2 Moisten the broken edges and stick them back together. Put the mint back in the packet.

3 Put another, uncracked, mint in your right-hand pocket, along with a cloth or large handkerchief.

Trick time

Give them the string and ask them to thread the mint onto it.

1 Take the special mint out of the packet and give it to someone in the audience.

2 Take the cloth and the uncracked mint out of your pocket. Keep this mint hidden in your right hand.

3 Drape the cloth over the mint on the string. Put both hands under the cloth, snap the trick mint and hide the pieces in your left hand.

The mint breaks silently because it's been broken before.

4 Hold the unbroken mint against the string with your right hand. Remove the cloth and broken mint with your left hand and put them in your left pocket.

5 Appear to pluck the whole mint off the string and hand it to the audience to examine.

Now how did she do that?

The magic bottle

Things you need

- Small glass bottle (preferably very dark glass)
- Pencil eraser
- Powder paint
- Magic wand (or thick pencil)
- Scissors

Surprise everyone by making a wand and a bottle hang in the air!

Get ready...

1. The bottle must be dark so nobody can see into it. If yours isn't, you can paint it on the inside.

2. To paint the bottle, mix up some powder paint and pour it inside. Put the lid back on and shake it about 50 times. Remove the lid and pour out the paint.

3. You can make a wand out of wooden dowelling or a very large pencil.

4. Cut a piece of rubber from the eraser. It must be about as big as a pea – just the right size to wedge itself between the bottle neck and the wand.

Trick time

Rubber in here.

1. Put the wand and bottle on the table. Hide the bit of rubber in your hand.

2. Pass the bottle to someone and ask them to make sure it's empty.

3 Take back the bottle. Give your friend the wand to examine, meanwhile slipping the bit of rubber into the bottle.

4 Put the bottle on the table, take the wand back and drop it into the bottle.

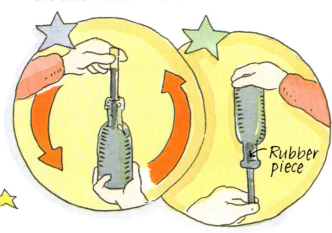

Rubber piece

5 Pick up the bottle and wand like this, and **very slowly** turn them upside down.

Make sure the rubber piece gets wedged between the wand and the neck of the bottle.

6 Let go of the wand. It's amazing – it doesn't fall!

Hide the rubber piece in your pocket!

7 Holding the wand and the bottle, slowly turn them upright again. Let go of the bottle – and it doesn't fall!

8 Give the wand a little push to release the rubber. Take the wand out and give it to someone to examine.

9 While they're looking at the wand, tip the bottle up and remove the rubber. Now give your friends the bottle to examine. Ask them to try the trick – and bet they can't do it!

The vanishing key

Things you need

Safety pin

Piece of elastic about 300mm long

Key

Two ways to make a key fly out of your hand and disappear.

Get ready . . .

1 Tie one end of the elastic to the key and the other to the safety pin.

2 Fasten the safety pin into your right sleeve, near the shoulder, so the key hangs down inside.

3 Adjust the length of the elastic so the key hangs out of sight, about 30mm up your sleeve.

4 Practise making the key vanish.

a Get hold of the key in your sleeve, using your left thumb and first finger. Pull the key out of your sleeve a little.

b Grasp the key with your right thumb and first finger. Keep the elastic hidden so the audience cannot see it.

c If you let go of the key, it should whizz back up your sleeve! Practise getting this right.

Trick one

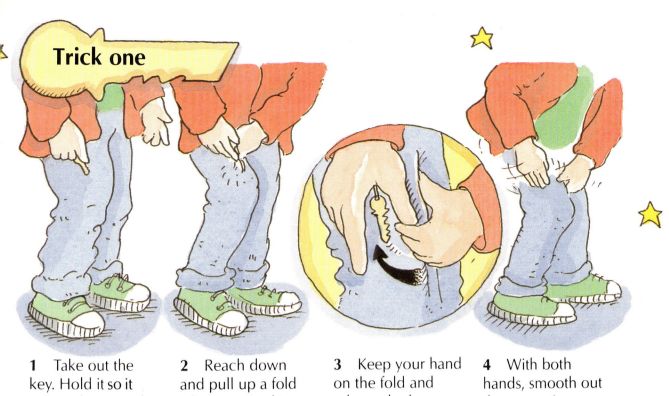

1 Take out the key. Hold it so it points downwards against your leg about 50mm up from your knee.

2 Reach down and pull up a fold of trouser or skirt material. Fold it up so it covers the key and hides it.

3 Keep your hand on the fold and release the key so that it secretly flies back up your sleeve.

4 With both hands, smooth out the crease in your trousers or skirt, and show that the key has vanished!

Trick two

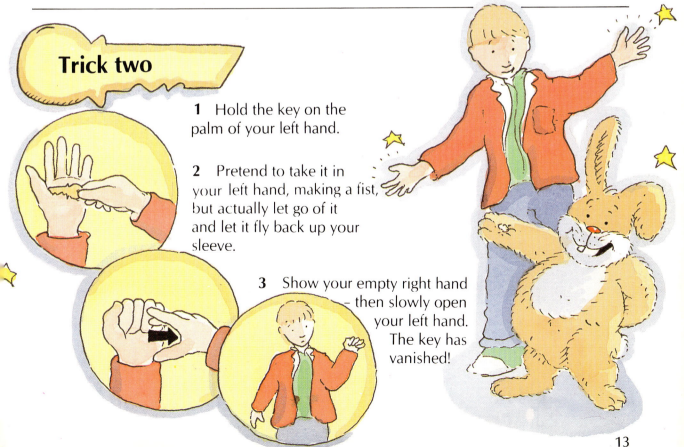

1 Hold the key on the palm of your left hand.

2 Pretend to take it in your left hand, making a fist, but actually let go of it and let it fly back up your sleeve.

3 Show your empty right hand – then slowly open your left hand. The key has vanished!

The floating pencil

Things you need

- Small glass bottle
- Pencil
- Blob of Blu-tack
- A very long hair **or** about 500mm of nylon 'invisible' sewing thread or very fine nylon fishing line

Make a pencil mysteriously jump up and down inside a bottle

Get ready...

A very long human hair works best in this trick, but if you can't get one use a very fine 'invisible' nylon thread.

1   Tie one end of the hair to a button on your jacket, blouse or shirt.

2   Wrap the other end of the hair round a small blob of Blu-tack and squash it in to fasten it securely.

Stick the Blu-tack to the end of the pencil.

Trick time

1   Hold the bottle in one hand. Drop the pencil in, Blu-tack end first.

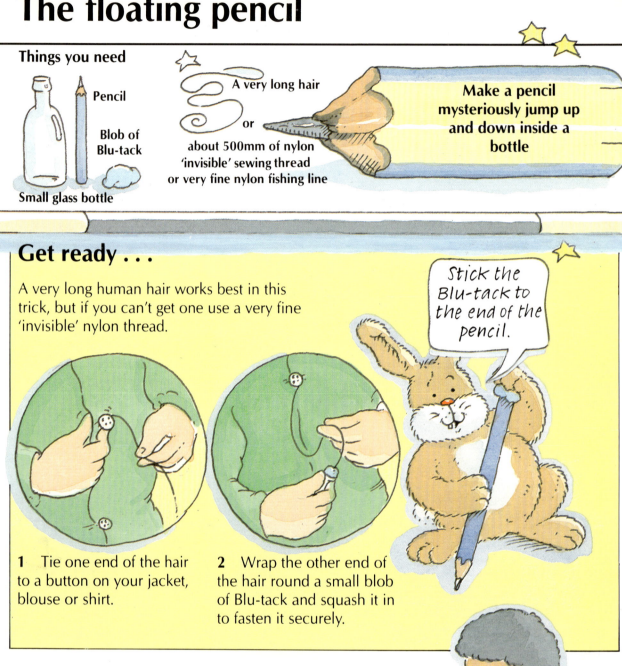

2 If you move the bottle back and forth, the pencil rises and falls very mysteriously.

3 Do this a few times then push the bottle even further forward. Now the pencil 'floats' out of the bottle.

4 Take the pencil in your free hand and reach out to offer it to the audience to examine.

5 As you stretch your arm, the Blu-tack comes off the bottom of the pencil and hangs, out of sight, on the end of the hair.

I bet nobody will be able to work out what makes the pencil move!

2 Keeping the box on the table, slide the tray out of the cover. Ask your friend to do the same.

3 Push the full tray back into the cover. Your friend must do the same.

4 Twist the box around one turn clockwise. Your friend does the same.

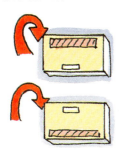 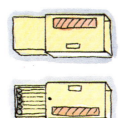 

5 Turn the box over completely. Your friend does the same.

6 Open yours a little at the dotted end. Your friend's box will be the wrong way up!

7 Ask the friend to adjust his or her matchbox so it looks like yours.

 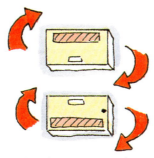 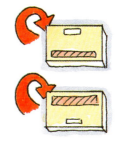

8 Close the boxes.

9 Twist them around one turn.

10 Turn them over completely.

11 Slide the tray out of your box – and your friend is wrong again!

This could go on all night – but your friend will always be wrong.

Reely tricky!

Things you need

- Cotton reel
- 2 pieces of string, each about 1 metre long

Remove a cotton reel from a piece of string without cutting the string.

Get ready...

It looks as if you're holding two separate pieces of string.

1 Fold the two pieces of string in half. Put one loop through the other, as in this drawing.

2 Hold the strings so that your fingers and thumb cover them where they are looped together.

Trick time

1 Holding the strings as shown above, pick up the cotton reel and let two ends of the string drop into the hole in the reel. If the ends of the string aren't stiff enough to drop easily into the hole, bind them with sticky tape before you start the trick.

As you pull, hide the looped part in your fingers.

3 Gently feed the strings through until the looped part is inside the reel.

4 Take the strings by the ends and hold them loosely, with the reel threaded on. **Don't pull the strings.**

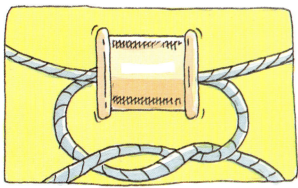

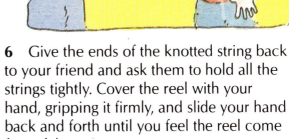

5 Ask a friend to hold the strings and reel. Tell them to give you two strings – one from each side of the reel. Tie these two strings together in a knot.

6 Give the ends of the knotted string back to your friend and ask them to hold all the strings tightly. Cover the reel with your hand, gripping it firmly, and slide your hand back and forth until you feel the reel come free of the strings.

7 Keep the reel covered by your hand. Carry on sliding your hand back and forward, then pull the strings slightly towards you and 'pluck' the reel off the strings. Your friend will be very surprised!

Magic bangle

Things you need

2 identical bangles or bracelets

Piece of string about 1 metre long

Jacket with inside pocket and wide sleeves

Make a bangle appear by magic on a piece of string tied between your wrists.

Get ready...

Put one of the bangles on your left arm and push it up your sleeve so it is hidden out of sight.

Hidden bangle

Trick time

1 Pass the other bangle and the piece of string to a member of the audience. Ask them to examine both carefully.

2 Ask someone to tie the ends of the string to your wrists as firmly as they can.

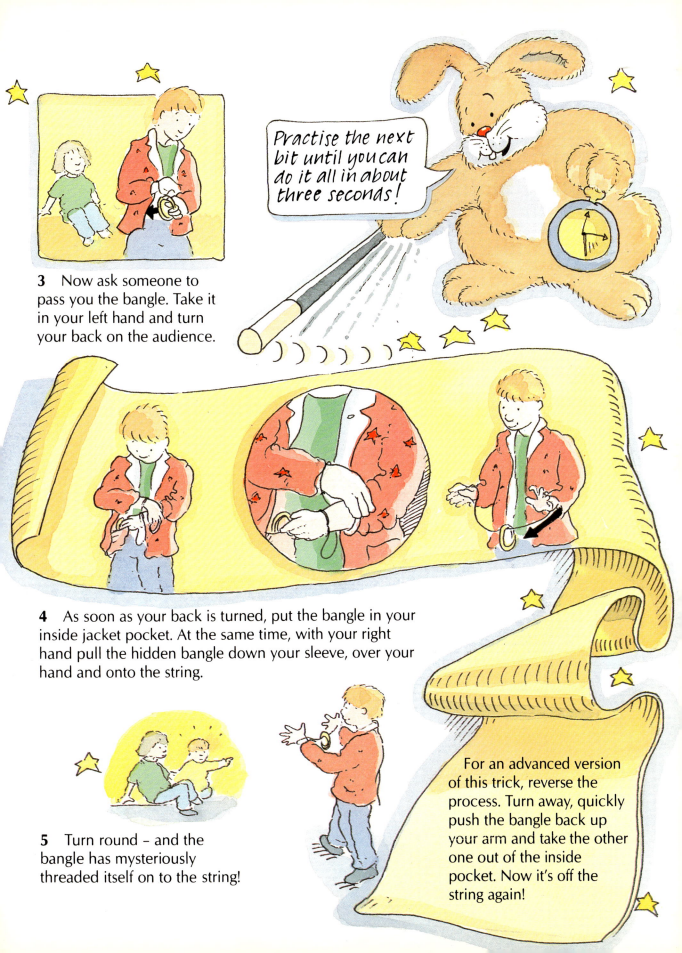

3 Now ask someone to pass you the bangle. Take it in your left hand and turn your back on the audience.

Practise the next bit until you can do it all in about three seconds!

4 As soon as your back is turned, put the bangle in your inside jacket pocket. At the same time, with your right hand pull the hidden bangle down your sleeve, over your hand and onto the string.

5 Turn round – and the bangle has mysteriously threaded itself on to the string!

For an advanced version of this trick, reverse the process. Turn away, quickly push the bangle back up your arm and take the other one out of the inside pocket. Now it's off the string again!

A knotty problem

Things you need

Piece of string about 1 metre long

Small piece of string about 150mm long

Sticky tape

Scissors

Cut a piece of string in two – then turn it back into one piece with no sign of any join.

Get ready...

1 Take the small piece of string and join the ends together to make a loop, using sticky tape.

2 Thread the long piece of string through this loop and put the whole thing into your pocket.

Trick time

It looks as if you're holding one long piece of string.

1 Reach into your pocket and take out the strings, making sure your fingers cover the sticky tape and the part where the loop and string are connected.

2 Hold the strings like this, take the scissors and cut through the loop.

3 Put the scissors down and tie the cut ends in a knot. Keep the loop hidden by your fingers.

The short string is now knotted around the long string.

4 Show everyone the cut and knotted string. Then take one end of the string in your left hand and with your right hand begin to wind it round your fingers.

The loop is in here.

5 As you wind it, the string goes through your right fist and you can secretly slip the knotted loop off it.

6 Put your right hand in your right pocket for your wand, dropping in the loop as you do so.

7 Wave the wand over your left hand, say some magic words, and begin to unwind the string from your hand.

8 Throw the string to your friends and let them examine it. There is no sign of a cut or a knot!

Finger on the pulse

Your fingernails are covered in tiny grooves. These grooves are the secret in this simple but surprising trick.

You will need

2 matches

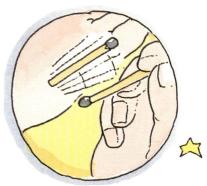

1 Hold a match firmly between your thumb and first finger. Press it down onto the nail of your second finger.

2 Put a second match on your left hand. Rest one end of it on the first match.

3 Press down hard on the first match so that it skids on the tiny grooves in your nail. This makes the second match jump.

Even when they are very close, your friends should not be able to see the first match move at all!

Ask a friend to hold your wrist while you do this trick. Tell them the match is jumping in time with their pulse.

Produced for Kingfisher Books Ltd
by Times Four Publishing Ltd

Kingfisher Books, Grisewood & Dempsey Ltd,
Elsley House, 24-30 Great Titchfield St, London W1P 7AD

First published in 1991 by Kingfisher Books

10 9 8 7 6 5 4 3 2

Copyright © Times Four Publishing Ltd 1991
All rights reserved
No part of this publication may be reproduced, stored in a retrieval system or transmitted by any means, electronic, mechanical, photocopying or otherwise, without the prior permission of the publisher.

Typeset by C-Type, Horley
Colour separations by RCS Graphics Ltd
Printed in Spain

BRITISH LIBRARY CATALOGUING IN PUBLICATION DATA
Day, Jon
   Let's make easy magic.
   1. Tricks
   I. Title   II. Fisher, Chris
793.8

ISBN 0-86272-718-9